Sneaky Animals

Wr...
Illus...

EGMONT

We bring stories to life

Book Band: White

Adapted from *The Ultimate Animal Criminals*
first published in Great Britain 2015

Sneaky Animals first published in Great Britain 2017
by Red Shed, an imprint of Egmont UK Limited
The Yellow Building, 1 Nicholas Road, London W11 4AN

www.egmont.co.uk

Text copyright © Egmont UK Limited 2015, 2017
Illustrations copyright © Sarah Horne, 2015, 2017

Consultancy by David Burnie

ISBN 978 1 4052 8494 3

A CIP catalogue record for this book is available from The British Library.

Printed in China
65793/1

The publisher would like to thank the following for permission to reproduce
their material. 6l E.O./Shutterstock; 7l Rudie Kuiter/OceanwideImages.com;
7r Brandon Cole Marine Photography/Alamy

Stay safe online. Any website addresses listed in this book are correct
at the time of going to print. However, Egmont is not responsible for content
hosted by third parties. Please be aware that online content can be subject
to change and websites can contain content that is unsuitable for children.
We advise that all children are supervised when using the internet.

Series and book banding consultant: Nikki Gamble

Sneaky Animals

Reading Ladder

Contents

Introduction

Not all animals play by the rules and many have developed clever ruses to get their own way. Some are good at disguising themselves to sneak up on prey. Others turn to thievery or become con artists to get food. Read on to find out how they live – or die.

Masters of disguise

Roll up! Roll up! Come and see those who copy the actions or the looks of others for their own devious ends.

Caterpillars are popular snacks for many creatures, including birds and rodents. Some caterpillars disguise themselves as scary snakes to hide from predators.

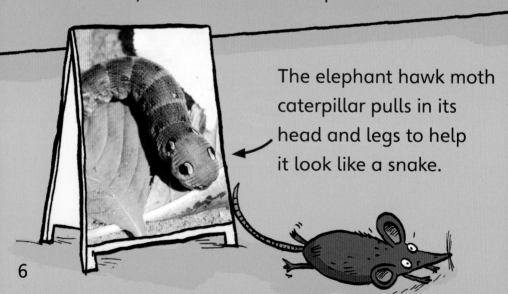

The elephant hawk moth caterpillar pulls in its head and legs to help it look like a snake.

The mimic octopus is truly clever at disguising itself to escape danger or catch prey. Here are two of its many camouflages.

Camouflage 1

The octopus bundles most of its arms together. It lets one arm trail behind to look like a stingray.

Camouflage 2

To appear as a poisonous sea snake, it changes colour, creating the snake's yellow and black bands.

Fake appeal

Some animals look so cute that we cannot believe they would do any harm. But many are deadly, vicious or violent!

The slow loris hangs about in the rainforests of southeast Asia, snacking on insects, fruit and leaves. Its large eyes make it very appealing, but it has a deadly bite.

Slow loris

Venom is stored in patches by its elbow that the loris licks. The venom mixes with its saliva and one bite may cause death.

Poison dart frogs are found in Central and South American rainforests. They are very pretty and come in a dazzling array of colours. They are protected by very poisonous skin.

Poison dart frog

The poison strength varies from species to species. Some frogs have enough venom to kill an adult human!

Animal assassins

This sinister selection of watery assassins sneak up on their prey and use unexpected deadly weapons to stun, kill and destroy.

The Archerfish fires little pellets of water out of the roof of its mouth. These can knock insects up to 5 metres away off their perches in the trees and into the water where the fish can eat them.

Archerfish

A pistol shrimp snaps its giant claws shut with great force. This creates a powerful blast of pressure that travels at speeds of up to 100 kilometres per hour to stun, or even kill, a small fish.

Pistol shrimp

The shock from an electric eel can knock over a horse or kill an alligator.

Electric eel

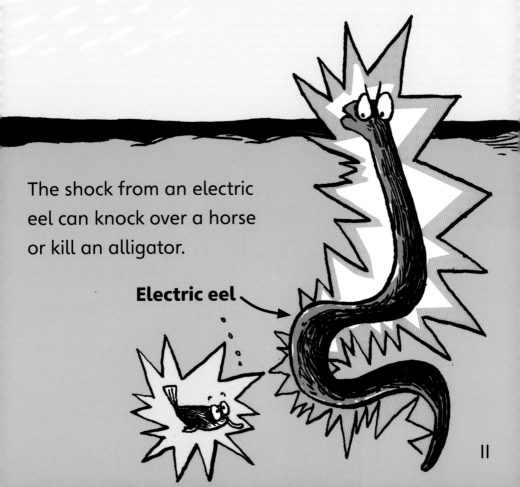

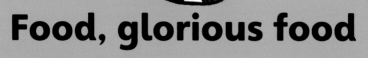

Food, glorious food

Hunger drives some tricky critters to an assortment of crimes to satisfy their rumbling tummies. They slip in to steal food when no-one is looking, or brazenly commit daylight robbery!

Ring-tailed lemur

Cicada

Some creatures steal food moments after others have done all the hard work collecting it. Seabirds such as skuas and frigatebirds filch fish caught by other seabirds, often in mid-air.

White gull

Frigatebird

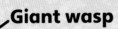

Giant wasp

On the island of Madagascar, a ring-tailed lemur waits until a giant wasp stings a crunchy cicada and drags it off to its underground lair. Just as the wasps are preparing to eat, the lemur steals the cicada.

13

Squatters' rights

Some underhand creatures break and enter. Their aim may be to help themselves to food or take over another creature's home completely.

Cuckoo

A cuckoo will visit another bird's nest, push out one of the eggs and lay one of its own instead. Once hatched, the baby cuckoo pushes out other eggs or baby birds from the nest so it can get all the food.

The burrowing owl steals the burrows of prairie dogs, armadillos or tortoises because it doesn't want to dig its own. The owl takes over the nest and then sees off the original owner!

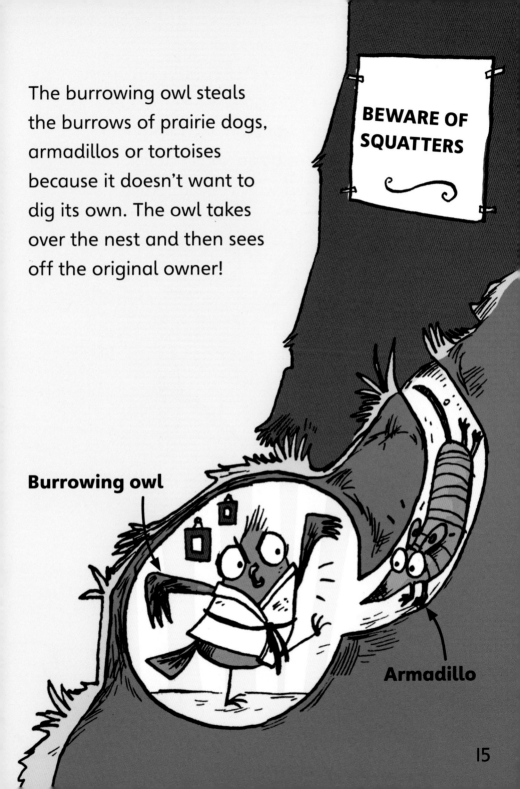

BEWARE OF SQUATTERS

Burrowing owl

Armadillo

A kangaroo in the Czech Republic escaped from his owner and hopped around helping himself to underwear from washing lines. Benji, a two-year-old roo, was finally caught red-handed with frilly knickers!

Stop thief!

Not all animal thievery is about food. Some tricky animals just spot something they fancy and take it, much to the surprise of the owner!

Californian cat Dusty is the reigning king of kitty kleptomania (repeated stealing). He's stolen more than 600 items so far!

Dusty's swag bag includes:

213 towels

73 socks

40 balls

18 shoes

8 bathing suits

2 frisbees

1 stuffed dinosaur

No escape

Some varmints work in wild groups to either defend themselves or heap misery on others. They work as a team to ambush and kill prey.

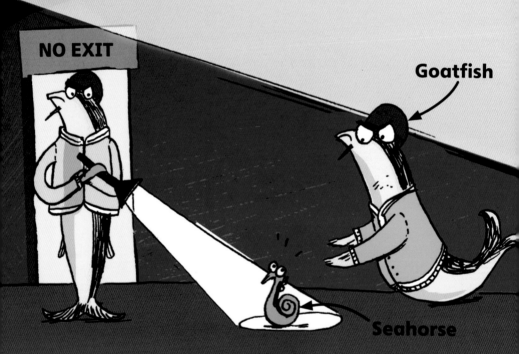

NO EXIT

Goatfish

Seahorse

One tropical goatfish swims after a seahorse while others in the group seal off the escape routes. The goatfish swap roles so that everyone gets a go at chasing and eating.

In the South American rainforest, coatimundis ambush prey such as the green iguana, which is three times their size.

Coatimundi

Green iguana

Some of the coatimundis climb a tree to scare the iguana, making it leap to the forest floor, where the rest of the gang lie in wait!

Con artists

There are some real confidence tricksters in the natural world. These deceitful creatures fool other living things to get food or to defend themselves.

Blanket octopus

Con 1

The blanket octopus spreads out the webbing between its arms to look like a giant red cape. This makes it look much bigger and scares away many predators.

A broken-rays mussel has a fishy lure on its shell that moves in the ocean currents. When a sea bass gets close, the mussel fires a cloud of larvae (young). These attach to the bass to grow and travel away from their parent.

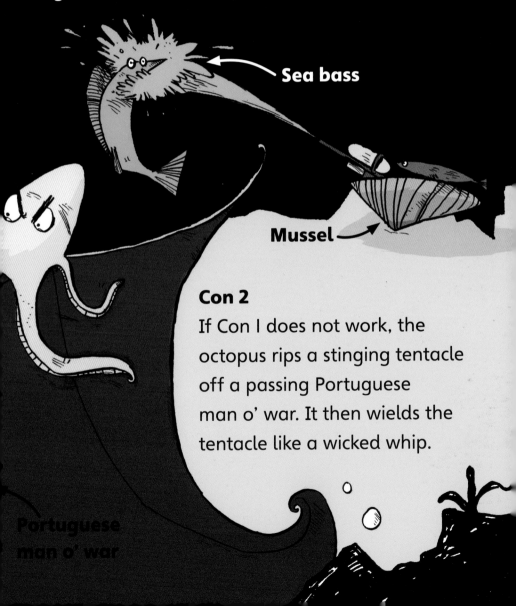

Sea bass

Mussel

Con 2
If Con I does not work, the octopus rips a stinging tentacle off a passing Portuguese man o' war. It then wields the tentacle like a wicked whip.

Portuguese
man o' war

Gangster rule

Meet the cane toad, one of nature's mobsters and hoodlums. These slippery desperados find many devious ways to take over the neighbourhood.

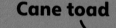

Cane toad

The biggest ever cane toad measured 38 centimetres long and weighed over 2.6 kilograms. Big trouble!

About 100 cane toads were first taken to Australia from Hawaii in 1935 to eat the cane beetles that were destroying the sugar crop. Today there are more than 200 million of them in Australia.

Cane toads are toxic. They have severely reduced the populations of other Australian animals, such as this quoll.

Quoll

Monkey business

Everyone loves a mischievous monkey but some sly characters take it too far. Meet the clever creatures that can make a monkey out of humans.

In safari parks, rhesus macaque monkeys and baboons have been known to hop onto moving cars and grab a free ride. They also rip off car aerials, hubcaps or windscreen wipers.

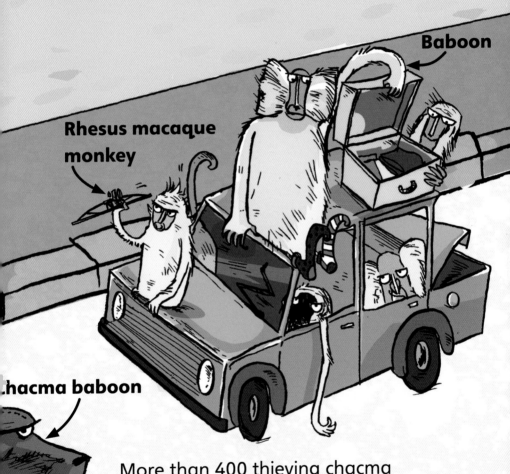

Baboon

Rhesus macaque monkey

hacma baboon

More than 400 thieving chacma baboons prowl the streets of Cape Town, South Africa. They clamber up apartment blocks, breaking through windows on the hunt for food.

Breakout!

Some animals in captivity might dream of freedom, but only a few really slippery critters escape! A handful manage to stay on the run for months.

Escape I

In 1935, a worker at the Jungle Camp Animal Park in New York, USA, left a wooden plank across a water-filled moat. Capone, a rhesus monkey, led more than 170 monkeys out of the zoo.

ZZZZZ

SECURITY

Escape 2

In the late 1990s and early 2000s, there were 35 animal breakouts from Los Angeles Zoo, USA. A female gorilla called Evelyn made five of these, once standing on the back of another gorilla, called Jim.

Escape 3

In 1958, Cyril, a sea lion, broke out of a zoo in Canada and managed to swim across the Canada–USA border. After 11 days, he was recaptured 640 kilometres away from the zoo.

Lethal line-up

These terrifying creatures sneak up on humans! Although most animals do so out of fear or for self-defence, there are a fearsome few that go on the attack.

OVER 400 VICTIMS

OVER 30 VICTIMS

The Champawat Tiger (left) was a Bengal tigress that killed 400 people in Nepal and India in the 1890s. The two lions dragged railway workers out of their tents in Africa in 1898.

This killer Nile crocodile, called Gustave, is thought to be over 60 years old and to have killed more than 300 people. He lurked in Lake Tanganyika and the Ruzizi river, central Africa, but has not been seen since 2008.

WANTED

OVER 300
VICTIMS
SO FAR

Glossary

burrow   A hole or tunnel dug by an animal usually to make a home or use as a food store.

crop   A plant that is grown deliberately by farmers to produce either food or another product, such as fibres to make clothing.

hatch   When a bird or other creature emerges from its egg.

insect   A small creature with six legs and a body formed of three parts: the head, a middle section (thorax) and the abdomen.

larvae   Newly hatched babies or the young form of creatures.

Fun facts

Shoplifter Akira, a Siberian husky dog, thought nothing of trotting more than nine kilometres to steal bones from butchers' shops.

moat   A deep ditch, sometimes filled
              with water.

predator   A creature that hunts and feeds
              on other creatures.

prey   A creature that is hunted or caught
              for food.

saliva   Liquid that is produced in the mouth
              to help soften and wet food before
              it is swallowed.

species   A group of related animals.
              Individuals in a species can breed
              with each other to produce young.

toxic   Acting as a poison.

venom   Poison that, if injected into the
              body of a living thing, can cause
              harm or death.

Chinstrap penguins build
nests out of stones. But
some of these sneaky
birds nip over to help
themselves to stones from
their neighbours' nests!

Index